Eh Tih Zwell

Poems by
Kezia Sproat

Eh Tih Zwell

Poems by
Kezia Sproat

Skye's The Limit
Publishing and Public Relations

Galena, Ohio, United States of America

Eh Tih Zwell — Poems by Kezia Sproat

©2019 by Kezia Sproat. All rights reserved.
Paperback re-issue 02-20-2020

keziasproat.blogspot.com

Published by *Skye's The Limit Publishing & Public Relations, LLC*
PO Box 133, Galena, Ohio 43021
(ph) 740-913-1439 | (fax) 740-548-4929
stlpublishing.com

Cover and interior design by White Plum Creative, LLC
Cover photos by Kenneth Breidenbaugh, used with permission.

This book may not be reproduced in whole or in part, in any form or by any means, electronic or mechanical, including photocopying, recording, or by any information storage and retrieval system now known or hereafter invented, without written permission from the publisher and/or author.

Books published by Skye's The Limit Publishing & Public Relations, LLC may be available at special discounts for bulk purchases in the United States by corporations, institutions, and other organizations. For more information, please contact the Marketing Department at info@stlpublishing.com

Published in the United States of America, Ohio, Galena.

ISBN-13: 978-1-939044-44-0 (paperback)

ISBN-13: 978-1-939044-43-3 (hardcover)

PUBLISHER'S NOTE

Every possible effort has been made to ensure that the information contained in this book is accurate at the time of going to press, and the publisher and author cannot accept responsibility for any errors and omissions, however caused. No responsibility for loss or damage occasioned by any person acting, or refraining from action, as a result of the material in this publication can be accepted by the editor, the publisher, or the author.

Acknowledgements

"Driving Up from Piketon" appeared as three poems in *Write On!: A Book of Poems for the Women's Poetry Workshop 25th Anniversary Celebration*, Columbus: Northwood ArtSpace, April 4, 2000.

"The Limb of the Earth: Three Poems By and For Laurel Clark" appeared as one poem in Bettyann Holtzman Kevles, *Almost Heaven: The Story of Women in Space*, Cambridge, MA, Perseus Books Group, 2003. Micki Seltzer, a charter member of Women's Poetry Workshop, suggested we honor Laurel Clark's memory by arranging lines from her space-to-earth e-mails. The spaceship Columbia was destroyed on reentry in January 2003.

Contents

Poems 1

Gentrification..3
Before the Pennsylvania Primary 5
Driving Up From Piketon...................................7
The Report 9
An Entrance to the Time of Peace........................11
A Snake 13
The Panther 15
As With These Lengthening Years........................17
To Bruce Lombardo on His Way to Heaven 19
September 12, 2001 21
September 11, 2002 23
September 11, 2003: The Pendulum at Shawnee State......25
Brahms Saves Lives in Circleville 27
At Highbank: American Patriots 29
Elegies for Millie 31
Mother's Birthday...35
Heaviness & Weight 37
Our New House..39
Status Maintenance, Northern Hemisphere, 2001.........41
A Challenge: Columbus as Port William 43
Second Exercise for Wendell Berry Fans 45
Ellin Carter at Highbank Farm, 1964.....................47
Pike Heritage Players..49
Women's Poetry Workshop 51

For E. F. Schraeder	53
On Behalf of All Educators	55
My Cousin Skip	57
What Else I Remember	59
Memorial Salad	61
For a Friend Whose Mother Taught	63
The Limb of the Earth: Three Poems by and for Laurel Clark	65
Thin Threads	67
Olentangy Village Pool	69
The Heart with Skill to Listen	71
Internet Morality Soup	73
The Next Time	75
Why We Read Fiction	77
How We Are Now	79
Masterpieces of World Literature in Translation	81
A Song for Hall House*	83
Away from the Mess	85
Listening	87
The Hopewell	89

Notes   91

Also by Kezia Sproat   93

Eh Tih Zwell

2 Eh Tih Zwell

Gentrification

With no idea how the story ends
I sit here writing Valentines
wrapped in uncoordinated layers
Just like the "old ladies" we used to laugh at
And proud of it.
Then I was young, loud, obnoxious
patronizing my neighbors
with home improvement
The electrical truck outside all day
five brush removals
plumbing, new furnace, knocked-out walls.

Now how proud I am of having been here 24 years,
and a new generation of young brash mothers
(20 of them!) come to the Garden Club I started and
Tell me what would be best
and pity me for being afraid to come to meetings
when the ground is covered with ice.

Northwood Park, Columbus, 1994

4 Eh Tih Zwell

Before the Pennsylvania Primary

Running west from Waverly
in a shiny red saddle on an old red horse,
Ahead, an anomaly in the wide left
(really on the far right)
double left turn lane off U. S. 35
Enormous lumps seem to be moving alone.

Closer in, a red SUV pulls them. They dwarf it.
Turning onto 104, now closer beside them
the lumps morph to coffins, three in a row.
Chilly death? No
Finally, they are sofas
lined up loosely, tied together
going to be sat on
at the SUV's home.

They will swallow up
the driver and his children
hers, theirs, everyone who sinks in them.

High definition will reach deep inside them
(flat screens appearing innocent
only pretending slyly to save them).

They will sit for hours and days and years
in those soft coffins, waiting
for something significant

to happen before them.
They think they will see the vote, not the sneer
the slow smothering, the damp and cold
dancing that is not a dance, never was a dance.

Eh Tih Zwell

Driving Up From Piketon

In memoriam John I. Vanmeter, III

Sunday night, Cornelia tells us
Look at that cloud, one dark above another,
See the dark as a mountain, the other fog.
Columbus is in high mountains, overshadowed by
  high ones.
Louring too close to the city.
Or, it can be a tidal wave.
Makes driving more interesting.

Cherokee wagons on the Trail of Tears.
In my new red Oldsmobile,
I must now imagine.
Give back, go back, to 1801.

Give thanks to the Lord
for this much of the day.

Flemish painters all drew distant hills blue
near ground yellow brown,
middle distance clean green.
Before us on a hill east of Adena
sits Evening, fine as by a Flemish master.
Huge round new hay bales rolled and rapt on it:
a flock of great sheep, soft, cool, brown, round
quiet on a pure green twilight hill.

You and your strong sisters
scratched and pulled square bales
once onto wagons
helping farmhands
in the summer heat
gathering in then
as we are gathered now
between home and this same river.
You and I, rolled bales and ready
tucked in for the night,
for the morning
the comforting hills still
blue but not distant.

Thank God every straw,
every point of the day.

It's OK. Porches always fall first
faces sag too, brains cloud,
psyches droop, and it all falls.

Later, the house, thick stone, will
come back, the wall stand
solid, true to its brother wall, angles
right, and deemed in fashion.

Children unheard, undreamed of
sleep safe when the winds come roaring,
the sky blackens, corn lies flat in the field.
The wall will stand between
the West and its young.

Years or centuries later

Someone may come, build another porch,
the house still there, OK with the new
as with the old, as unbent as
Horatio, were
the plays of Shakespeare reinterpreted.

The Report

At the end of Chopin's ninth nocturne
a child hears sudden gunfire
close, then in the distance

He asks us to listen,
twice, three times.
Now it comes closer.

Someone runs from one building to another
and doesn't make it.
His brother must run too,

Stops in silence at his brother's body,
but makes the next shed
before the guns report again.

I practice this nocturne
for my mother's friend who wants to hear it.
I do the gunfire

More and more proficiently
as if I were Dr. Strangelove
I ride bombs to the ground.

Chopin will die of tuberculosis, later.
But he has told this tale
and I must listen.

10 Eh Tih Zwell

An Entrance to the Time of Peace

Fire flowers southwest, due west.
Sun feeds fuchsia

controlling my whole picture
only tiny dots for darkness and pain

Yet, below a triangle—the shape of stability—

In the center floats an entrance to the time of peace,
the days of balance.

Green kimonos draped,
Green, a color of relief, a color of rest,

the green of an old silk kimono
I found in a closet and kept for seventy years

Sometime to be displayed upon the wall.

Eh Tih Zwell

A Snake

Innocent, small, gracefully curving
in a good sweet wave on the kitchen floor
of the country house
but all I could see then
were spots on his back making
the Great Guide Anxiety
Ruler Especially of This Universe
foresee its finding a compatriot and mating all winter,
leaving countless little copperheads
to grow up just beneath the old floors
then pop out in silence some night
and kill us humans all. Were that the case

We would not die softly, nor would this snake.
A serrated spatula, shaped to cut quiches and lift
them steamingly onto well-set plates, was
my murder weapon.

God of All Snakes forgive me
I cut the little one in two just behind the head
right there on the floor, instantly
he opened his mouth in a wide-open silent scream
of pain that hurts me still. a month later remembering.

God of all Fears, God of all Anxieties,
Leave us, please.
Give us again strength
True One
simply to pick up and put snake babies back outside.

Eh Tih Zwell

The Panther

Going south to the Ohio
a panther stopped me
long-tailed, black, dying
stretched by the road,
rare and beautiful.

I hurried north calling the ancestors
"Come, for the panther is dead and
we must mark his life."

In a long procession of carriages they all came
making a circle, humming softly
each in turn asking for data:

"Had you kits, panther?"
"What path did you follow here?"
"Were you alone?"

and so on until the panther spoke, saying
"Do not mind me here.
Stop blowing, cease whining.
Be still, still and only listen."

16 Eh Tih Zoell

As With These Lengthening Years

Look out the window.
Try to count pine needles,
or follow birds,
or make the wind change
to a breeze.

Humbled, rejoice in long effort and failure.
So you can't do it. Think what fun
it was to think about it, stretching,
then plan a way for something else,
something you can do

Like a good breakfast for your firstborn
sleeping in your house right here
the first new day of the millennium

Or a birthday cake for your friend
drinking coffee not too far away

Or a project to help a sad child smile
a suicidal orphan hope
or anyone see

where the herons come to raise their children.

To Bruce Lombardo on His Way to Heaven

Dear Lamp,

When we read about it

My old black dog lay
howling on the kitchen floor,

stretched out. Stasis.

Dear Shining Lamp,

Judy Coleman's calico cat
went yesterday to welcome,
To welcome you, Lamp.

Children pretending to be rhinos
And the rhinoceros herself,

The Great Mother Rhinoceros
And her pack of wild dogs

Dance to receive you,

Their Brother and Our Lamp,

Away across the wide wide water.

20 Eh Tih Zwell

September 12, 2001

From a south window in a house of ruin
an early line
of light along the ground,

a shaft of sun
a spear of brightness
crosses under pines.

Morning slices through the orchard
where no orchard is, but was.

Still, an orchard blooms
and feeds
hummingbirds of memory.

22 Eh Tih Zwell

September 11, 2002
Highbank

Another hawk soared this morning
We walked to the river,
We came back for the Reading of Names.

A mile of ten-foot corn
stalks still green
ears gold, white
each scarved in brown silk,
come back for the Reading of Names.

Hawk-brother, lazy as ever,
relaxed on the updraft
played with the wind
as hawks may
as a hawk can
come back for the Reading of Names.

WVXU Cincinnati
the day full of color
pinks of east reflect west

Five hundred greens stripe the horizon
helping blues
as many textures in the hills

One drip of rain at dawn
a little wind, just a little
where a Shawnee warpath
runs the other side
We came for the Reading of Names.

We came back

Eh Tih Zwell

September 11, 2003:
The Pendulum at Shawnee State

In my next life I
would like
to understand mathematics.

The coyote howls, lovely
as God on a summer evening

Sin theta - where theta is latitude
of any location-
times 360° gives the answer.

My old brown dog growls
in his sleep.
He hears the coyote

All three of us
lavishly privileged
on the evening.

Brahms Saves Lives in Circleville

Can't run like I used to, and keep seeing people I know
who belie the fiction I've achieved freshness
clean childlike naivete and simplicity
by leaving town and living in the country.

That round-faced tired black woman waiting for the
    bus in Columbus
I knew 50 years ago! Her hair still braided as we did then
behind the ears, folded tight on the head, in a circle,
like the German maidens in Riefenstahl's films.

A sign from God:
Eine Deutsches Requiem on WOSU-FM as I drive home
forty-six miles in the mist and rain,
now fifty feet in the air, terrifying fast
construction zone
a window stuck half down.

Turn up the volume.

No one can bother me, no slander touch me.
We sang it in the Vassar Choir, 1959
with the Julliard Orchestra.
Edicts of Nature proclaim if you've been part of that
(even if you sang in English)
no one can ever bother you again.
You have medicine and power.

Live to make it happen in the smallest, nastiest,
    most frightened
scrunched up minds and hearts you can possibly find
or that will certainly find you.
The announcer, long-lived deep velvet
celebration of God, Bob Conrad
The conductor, George Szell
The year, 1969
The orchestra, of course, Cleveland.

Eh Tih Zwell

Hello, Slander, Deceit, Libel
Liar, Worm or Devil.
Good evening. Welcome!
I laugh beside you lovingly.
I pat your fanny in friendship.
Don't bother trying to touch me, because
Brahms and my buddies conquered Death itself.
I know how to help them
and teach you too.

At Highbank: American Patriots

1. K. V. Sproat

Fall in the air already
tomatoes not ripe
I worry. *The Christian Science Monitor*
shows Railway Children in Mumbai
(Bombay in fancy shops)
Many have polio. I toss nights
sleep in day, sink slowly
consumed by bamboo tables, brass lamps
comfortable hand-dyed Indian cottons
that need no ironing.

Have you noticed the lovely colors
(now often seen on the Newshour)
worn by the refugees in Darfur?
So bright and various, they would go well.
they could be a trend
draped on the runways next season.
I read Woodward, Friedman, Suskind
pray every 30 minutes
give all I have to the Kerry campaign
barely feed my dog.

2. Vincent Williams

If my knee hurts I whine and take aspirin.
He was a distant grandfather.
Too lazy to learn how many greats back,
I give him superficial notice in this poem.
He sits above a mirror on the mantle
balanced between a prehistoric rock hammer
and an abandoned oriole's nest.
Images tell nothing. This man
looks very nerdy, but nothing about him was.
He fought with Washington, and lived long
enough after to sit for a daguerreotype.

Elegies for Millie

1.

Whatever you say, bird, and
Good and loud, jenny wren or warbler
Whoever you are,
Tell us this morning, here.

Hear! Hear!
On this porch that once was ours,
Loudly claimed by you now.

The old black dog that jumped six feet
Not twenty from this spot
Leaping for thrown balls
Like trout for a fly
Her spine twisting
Impossibly high
Turning in mid-air for the catch
Like you, even a bird

Waits now for me to signal, and
The brown dog to watch
For Death.

She can't stand now
But you can sing.
Let's hear it now, good and loud,
Small bird, big voice.
Tell us about it.

2.

So many times I worried in winter
disappearing at the end of a walk.
Not long ago, the snow knee-deep
frozen over, crust-topped, dark
coming on, I, no boots
or means to sleep in the house
You, down in the trackless woods.
I saw you go.
Calling back and forth along the ridge
till I could call no longer,
my feet frozen and wet
how I worried about your dying
injured or alone or attacked by coyotes
imagined calling the Queen boys, the Sheriff
to helicopter in to look for an old black dog
injured and helpless in the deep woods.
Then just at dark, typically, you came trotting out
calm as could be, your mission accomplished,
back to your loyal assistant, this willing servant
to the genius ball-catcher of all time.

3.

At last it was just the opposite. Four solid days of
canned dog food in the hospital, lots of stroking,
telephone consults, the finest doctor's finest care
her loving assistants, steroids, for five days.
You finally lifted your head to drink.

"You have a difficult decision to make," said the vet.
I knew what it had to be. We made an appointment.
You could still lick the brown dog's face
You could still hold your head and look at me
but not stand, not walk, never jump
except in memory, in photographs where you are
    jumping
and the delighted visiting children
not believing how a dog could catch balls
until they saw you

So after a while I said, "We're ready.
She's ready but I'm not." I cried in a corner chair
while the vet and her assistant, sitting with you on the
    floor
lovingly cradled you in their arms
your black fur glistening. "She's gone," one said.

Before I could think more or feel
(Those born during war can disavow feeling)
I took you to the farm and dug a grave.
Helping for a wedding that day,
The bride's brother threw in the first shovel of dirt.

I can see your grave from the kitchen and
I can plant flowers and
I still see you jumping
So can the children.

Mother's Birthday

The trees now like brides don white dresses in spring,
then slowly take them off for green ones,
working to produce, produce, oxygen and fruit
and babies, good working women
married to the earth.

Will they win the war this time?
Are they desperate and determined,
as you were then, as I am now?
Do they know the earth is dying?

Eh Tih Zwell

Heaviness & Weight

June 12, 2003, hope of peace almost dead
like 1948, 1949, 1950, 1951, 1952, 1953,
1954, 1955, 1956,1957, 1958,
1959, 1960, 1961, 1962, 1963, 1964,
1965, 1966, and the next long 40 years.

A learned guest wants one leader to be killed,
says it with acid anger as if that helped
and seems to believe it really would help and
even says she's said it a lot but no one kills him
as if people should barge out and kill someone to suit her
then sits back comfortably as if among intelligentsia
saying saying saying (lofty assurance)
peace is impossible
Posing as wise, posing, posing as learned
posing as knowing
No-ing no-ing noing noing noing.

Pseudo-wise newspeople paid for pronouncing, no-ing
Mothers cry on both sides, on all five sides, on all six
    sides,
seven, eight, nine, ten, eleven, twelve, thirteen

My 5-year-old grand-nephew understands infinity.
We named the southwest terrace for him
on the morning of our firstborn's wedding
with old old ideas in the ceremony and
even older ideas than humans have held
manifested when an ancient magnolia limb
wide, strong, grey, bent steeply down to help
its brother olive trees
aiming right through the earth
to cure the old ideas.

Fathers cry on both sides, on all five sides, on all six sides,
Seven sides. eight, nine, ten. eleven. twelve, thirteen,
 twenty thousand sides.
Today a bomber dressed as his enemy was just that, not
 just dressed as,
but was (exactly, fully) because God came here, saying
an eleventh commandment, "You are what you wear."
and then a twelfth, "You are what you say."
You are the very words of your own mouth: all of them.
Every word that comes from your mouth is you.
Every year of sorrow that you live.
Every day and every hour.
Sisters cry on all sides, all twenty thousand ...
children... no-ing.

Our New House

Run the film backwards through the camera
so these leaves of gorgeous brown and orange
of every yellow, the best tweed jacket of God,
float back to their waiting Mothers, the trees,
for a last hug, a last kiss of summer,
to celebrate our new house,
built on your best long plans, on the finest base,
and open to the hands—
four hundred at least—all firmly grasped
not one hand untouched.

Albert Gore, 11/2/1992, Port Columbus

Eh Tih Zwell

Status Maintenance, Northern Hemisphere, 2001

Purple myrtle blooms on Great-grandmother's grave this morning
(What an uplifting symbol! How provocative of sentiment!)
All over the cemetery people are trying hard
to be important, their stones and flowers just right.
By my sister's grave, I try to pull up a dead boxwood
but the ground is suddenly frozen.

In Zimbabwe a woman named Cathy has been run off
the farm where she was born.
She writes e-mail, imploring for help
to stop starvation in her beloved country.
The invading multitudes don't know planting
nor have they a feel for harvest.
I read that in yesterday's *Monitor*.

The story already told in *Disgrace* by cold Mr. Coetzee
who stood just to shake my hand last month, the friend
who introduced us having said I knew something of Shakespeare.
So important at that moment, I told my daughters and friends
and—frail to the last—I drive through the graveyard vaguely wondering
where will I be buried and what the stone will say.

In Afghanistan, while we slept last night, George Washington
Thomas Jefferson Kofi Annan John and Abigail Adams
began something truly important,
a set of rules, a way of going, a plan for civility
based on something beyond self-importance.

The living are more important than the dead, need
more than red, white, and purple uplifts in cemeteries.
God be praised. Mr. Karzai calls the same and only Allah
All together now
Now we bow
our hands in prayer.

A Challenge: Columbus as Port William

The old barber in Kentucky, fiction though he was
Loved a little hometown to the point of seeing it heaven
Peopled it, kept it going through three novels at least
Through generations of mostly farmers
Uncles, wives, lovers, barns, pastures
Mystic visions borne of love

Port William, safe haven, contrast with all the world
Especially Louisville, especially San Francisco, no where
    else
Worthy and perfect, no purer people, kinder friends,
For the barber, the writer, solace and joy in its air.

And then Columbus. What shall we do in this place?
Try to love? Each one? The harried soccer mom
concerned with eyelash lengthening and the bureaucrat
of sniveling, can you love them? Work hard, now.

The angry, jealous outcomes of televised opulence
swaggering down High Street, football fanatics in
gray and red and red and grey and gray and red and noise
the whole crowd, the 95,000 yelling

[List the least lovable people imaginable here]

Love all? Does God? Can you?
Oh, give it a whirl.

Second Exercise for Wendell Berry Fans

Try it closer in
Try one block
One side of the street
One house
One person
Try, you.

Move out from there,
Far as you can
Then farther until
You even catch the arsonist.

Keep in touch.
Let me know
What you say.

46 Eh Tih Zwell

Ellin Carter at Highbank Farm, 1964

White pine we planted that year
have gathered together
closing the road to the graveyard.

You come, friend
challenging and
loving at once.

Gentle and sharp,
very sharp.

Now forty years
full of *observe*.

The snow came and left before
its talent at painting spruce, pine
and bare magnolia limbs was
caught for history.

So I wished more, and
immediately it came, steady as
fallen humanity,
beautiful as all virtue, all time
everywhere.

Eh Tih Zwell

Pike Heritage Players

Theatre is
an irritation of the skin
chronic and very contagious
you are never cured—

Thank God
for this epidemic.

50 Eh Tih Zwell

Women's Poetry Workshop
26th anniversary reading

We are the tall green stems
of the amaryllis
the blooms wilt.
We gather energy
from the sun
to store
in the bulb
to strengthen
the still-growing leaves.

Eh Tih Zwell

For E. F. Schraeder

Home from the Shakespeare Conference
(didn't think I could stay alert 12 hours, but I did)
Slept.
Woke at 1:00 am
Stacked pillows to read, but
never leaned back.

The Hunger Tree
sat me straight up
   on the edge
The birds, seeds in your garden
grabbed the tip of my brow
and cured that awful ego.

Thank you.

Eh Tih Zwell

On Behalf of All Educators

Burgess at Indianola:
sometime in the seventies.

Last week a sea lion jumped from its captivity water
to bite a child by the seat of her bloomers
and pull her in.

When your students got
"Word from above" they couldn't meet
at school on Saturday for a project—

they jumped out of that water
like a swarm of sea lions.

And for decades after,
looking again to talk with you
in a public park
or anywhere,
just anywhere.

Thanks, Jack!

My Cousin Skip

Organizes poetry readings,
Invites me,
Plans art shows,
Invites the world.
Has taught painting
for seventy years
to everyone who wants to take art
Some didn't know art was for their taking
but turned into giants and mountains when they found
  they could.

This for hundreds of people who show their work
  proudly,
smile inside, and visit the Metropolitan,
Their life-love, highly contagious.
When visiting Ross County, trustees of the finest
  museums
in the world fall at her feet, but she doesn't notice.

"See, this is how," she says, passing the canvas and paint.
"See, this is how," choosing food for her husband at
  market
"See, this is how," inviting strangers to eat venison
provided by a communications professor.
"Norm couldn't do stairs. We moved to a smaller house,
a Sears-Roebuck Norm had as a rental.
It was delivered by rail!"
From the porch, Norm waves and smiles
As happy as Buddha.

Still teaching painting,
pulling together all the parts of the world she loves
She walks to my car after their dinner party.
Among other thanks, I say, "I am very proud of you."
"What *for*?" she replies, and really doesn't know.
Too engaged in other matters,
not a moment for the sin of pride.

What Else I Remember
For Jackie

My first trips alone were
around the corner of Church and Chestnut
past the schoolyard to your house
to find a friend to play with.
Both of us yelled bigger and bigger lies to Chelsea Green
across Chestnut on Gerber. Your boyfriend was Duke
    Prince
who wrote you love letters all the time
I forget which one of our dads owned the whole
    hospital!
She was older. We had to impress her.
Next door now, her hair is white, as l write
professionals spray her lawn with fertilizer
Last year they blew dry cow manure
onto my terrace during a dinner party.
She was in Columbus. I forgave her, still
maybe feeling embarrassed for our big lies.

Your friendship made me a normal kid.
"How's the weather up there?" heard so often
I might have had a horrible height complex.

We were five when your Aunt Mary took us
to the Majestic to see *Snow White*.
I'm still terrified of the witch,
and lightning flashing on the mountain,
then walking home in a real downpour
not one on the screen, Aunt Mary constantly
telling me to hold my umbrella up
so it wouldn't poke your eyes.

Weekday mornings, your father walked past our house
dapper as Fred Astaire, smiling, vigorous, so kindly.
We went to the furniture store after school
bothering him at work, but he never acted bothered.
Your mother gave us soup and heart-shaped cut
    sandwiches in your kitchen on Church Street.

Best of all: Wondrous Sara, your tiny baby.
George so proud he glowed, in the tiny apartment,
like a real holy family, only a girl
and here in Chillicothe!

I have the green leather clutch purse
you sent forty-two years ago for graduation.
It doesn't wear out.
We painted our living room that same color
A cross between blue sky and pine trees.

I often visit George's grave at Grandview.
The way blocked yesterday by someone clearing brush for winter,
I went back to my family's plot,
Cleared brush there too.

Memorial Salad
*In memoriam, Ellin Eastwood Sucheston Carter,
Founder, Women's Poetry Workshop*

A couple of hours after getting the message
The evening of the day you died I made a salad:
Found in the back of the top shelf of the refrigerator,
the end of a jar of grape jelly
one and one-half olives in their brine
a little extra virgin olive oil
six cherry tomatoes from Highbank
some greens bought two weeks ago
green peppers grown at Highbank
"You know I love the place," you said

This all put together in anger and fury
sorrow and joy and gratitude
No one would force food into your mouth again
then watch it fall out

The grape jelly and olive brine, some cheese,
some chopped chicken, ingredients chosen in
Freedom thanks to Cathy's salad at the
WPW reunion at Highbank summer before last

No croutons so I toasted whole wheat
store-bought bread, twice, two slices.
When they came up, I held them tight
together and tore them in half,
then with my biggest knife made strips,
revolved them, made cubes, cutting, cutting,
cutting, cutting, angry, sorry for myself.

Stirred in vigorously with tears
but it made a damn fine salad for you.

For a Friend Whose Mother Taught

Having no proper paper or pen in the house,
snow covering every walk and tree,
I send you ancient Chinese sympathy
in ballpoint.

Not Old Chillicothe form,
but I trust your ability
to forgive the lapse
and maybe even laugh.

Five days before she left
the phone rang. I agreed
to teach math at the High School
the following Wednesday.

Often we see the forms
gathering, validating
celebrating, comforting.
Other times we can't.

Eh Tih Zwell

The Limb of the Earth:
Three Poems by and for Laurel Clark

Very busy doing
science round the clock
lightning spreading over the Pacific
the vast plains of Africa
the dunes on Cape Horn
rivers breaking through tall mountain passes
have seen my "friend" Orion several times
distributed to many
who I know and love

Hello
our magnificent planet
with the cityglow of Australia
the crescent moon setting
rivers breaking
the scars of humanity
a steep learning curve
Whenever
l do get to look out
lighting up the entire visible horizon

Above our magnificent planet
e-mail is precious
the continuous line of life
extending from North America
through Central America and
into South America.
This will be short.
Every orbit we go over
a slightly different part of the Earth.

Copied and arranged by
K.V. Sproat, March 29, 2003

Eh Tih Zwell

Thin Threads

Thin threads, thin threads
Society bound by thin threads

   1.

An elbow in line, or kindness among strangers
in a supermarket
Supermarket
world supermarket
ADM supermarket to the world

Mommy and Daddy to the world
smiling from the TV tube
Scowling at President Carter

Truth is never fit to tell
unless it fits our purpose well

We all know the Cubans are bad
as bad as we need them to be, whatever

Lies are fine and
truth is out of line.

Thin threads. the stewardess' sense of smell
saved three hundred
(Why does hate live so well?)

   2.

Let's get those grades!
Not the word of God,
not purple redbud in spring and a lover's smile,
but the acceptance letter from Harvard
is Heaven.

Daddy and Mommy love me
so thin threads, thin threads
I am a grade-point average

With portfolio. An award list.

The others were just people
like, the masses.
Now in my dorm room I look down
at my bleeding wrists

A word from the President
polysyllabic Latinate sounds
turning back into the mouths of bombers

Choking them

"They will only remember these bombs."
my friend lamented at the Writers' Retreat
during another war
twelve years ago.
He'd been in the Foreign Service forty years
sorrowfully looked at the ceiling
of the White Oak Inn as he spoke.

3.

Listen to the thin threads that bind

The mockingbird, blue bunting, swallow
The tiny fleeting kindness of a smile in the
copy-centered blank-filling classroom
is what should be graded.

Watch for that, John Ashcroft.

And I, pseudo-poet, pseudo-historian,
pseudo-moralist, pseudo-educator
now strive
(for, Elizabeth, I too am cursed, always striving
for something or grunting toward peace)
to identify bird songs and

cobwebs, thin threads of kindness
smiles like Kay Wolf's.

May 14, 2002
In memoriam, Elizabeth Shin, a Harvard suicide

Olentangy Village Pool

I hope the old people are dead now.
1 wouldn't want them to see this.
The owners spoke down the nose
I forget what they said I don't know them
It might have been inaccurate
the gist: unfortunate people live here, exclusively
those with few choices in life, economically speaking —
econ the only speech known by
the poor who have lots but want more money.

In this brown hole in the ground
was our element. We spent billions
thrilled two months ago
to find it on Mars.

At last year's healing
"'Hilling," Coach pronounced it, stern old Greek
opening, on the last day, his giant wit bag
a goodwill bag the size of Spain
(surprising, he'd seemed angry all summer)
beating our heads with flowers
in October, in Ohio
convulsing us with laughter
in the big pool. Exercising strangers
got to be friends (at the very least nodding in respect)
to go on at least another fifty years.

Hundreds maybe a thousand will fill
these dwellings on the raped river,
laugh before the bank slides down the flood.
Some may even grow old here
but I hope the ones I knew are dead and in mercy I
    hope it.

The new will be wonderful as well
but where will they find that out?

I wrote fifty poems swimming in that water.

The Heart with Skill to Listen

The heart with skill to listen
may have been broken
may have been mended
or never hurt, like the boy
who friended a bear
alone in the forest at three.

And lived, like the aloe plant in the window—
Cut, torn, used (and often)
to heal the cook's burnt fingers.

Growing always, growing always,
even a nuisance, even a weed

And the boy lived, amazing the sheriff
in a way sheriffs—accustomed to shock—
are never amazed, but they were that time.

Where did the bear's heart come from?
Where did it go?

Eh Tih Zwell

Internet Morality Soup

I used to be nonviolent
And love my fellow beings
Studied philosophy and religion too
Serioso, in my teens.

I rhapsodized about it
When the Internet was born
Wrote histories and poems!
So connected is the world

Good people write each other
understanding across borders
John Lennon's "Imagine" dream come true,
no more wars or boundaries

But the pablum friends keep sending
Has me spitting nails.

The Next Time

If there is a next time
I touch you,
here is what it will mean:

I risk my heart's
going from my body into yours
and walking around in it, dependently;
whether it will ooze into mist and fog
from me to you, or squeeze out through
the marrow bones of my toes and fingers,
I don't know, but
there it will go

leaving me altogether pallid
(unless I can grow another one),
calling on my hands and brain to follow it
about the world,
walking up and down in it,
seeing what to do for you next.

Eh Tih Zwell

Why We Read Fiction

For my mother, who didn't approve
whose prayer ended with its clogging things
thinking Truth so fine, various. glorious
as wind, flowers, then birds, then the Soil
who is Mother of us all, yes:

Like you, I wake in the night and think.
Guests coming soon, I re-arranged a shelf
in the upstairs bathroom, then some boxes
some racks in the closet, then this, then that
finally the floor, its rug soiled, is revealed.

It is night. very dark. All the lights are on.
Afraid of bats all the time, but coping.
I see the floor now, not clean enough
not by a long shot. I will need a bucket
that new lemon cleaner got against such a day

Such a revelation! I cross this floor nightly
My firstborn child walked on it in her wedding dress
(the one you made the year she was born and
it didn't fit that person but now fit her—perfect!)
Her sister. her great-hearted friend, both dressed
for ceremony and audience, walked on this damn dirty
   floor

I didn't know how it was until now
It was not godly glorious daytime
no birds, no shadows from trees
to distract from the Soil, but
fiction —Light—artificial as Edison could do
saved my day.

Eh Tih Zwell

How We Are Now

Believing all hosta like shade
Sum and Substance from Mr. Cory's
lived more than a year by the garage
under a volunteer redbud
close to a ginkgo trunk.

Proudest of all hosta,
he gasped toward the sun
weakened.
Just four meek leaves,
two eaten by bugs
cried each time I came in or went out.

At last to attend his weeping
I dug and carried him
with unceremonious respect
and a little optimism
(as we would a dead possum
in a plastic grocery bag)
eight long miles away.

(Mr. Cory, non-commital, pointed
with an elbow as he dug red day lilies
"There's a *Sum and Substance* in full sun!")

So you were plunked
in the brightest corner
of the south-facing farm garden.
Three weeks later

See, even this old torn leaf
all spots and holes
is getting bigger. It looks very bad
but we won't cut it because
it is still doing work.

The child asks, How? with her eyebrows.

Taking carbon dioxide from the air
converting sunlight to energy
moving it to roots for
new leaves
now already three.

Masterpieces of World Literature in Translation

Just divorced, lecturing in an old building
glancing out the door, I saw a god in the long hallway
investigating right and left but slowly walking toward
   my classroom.

Panic hit. Still lecturing, I prayed, "Lord, Help me!
A god appears headed for this classroom! Gird me, Lord!
with strength and calm to keep on teaching if he walks
   here.
I must feed my children. Compose me, Lord."

You enter, sit down; soon after you have to miss a class,
call me to apologize and learn what we did:
I tell you the whole *Odyssey* in one 45-minute phone call.
Mid-quarter, you return from Long Island enthusiastic
with Ram Dass' *Be Here Now*, then just out.
I assent. The whole class reads it.

We keep in touch. Later your engagement party—
I bring my children—and marriage to a nice girl.
Yes, I approve; letters after you finish graduate school
We keep in touch, then don't.

Athena to your Odysseus, thirty-six years later
I remove your collage inspired by Ralph Ellison's *Invisible
   Man*
from an old chest that must be shipped
immediately to Cairo, Egypt

Close enough to ancient Greece
where you and I now live.
Still here, brilliant, now more than ever timely,
I'm framing it to hang in my living room

Near the Picasso, which isn't really in the center
of the plastered-over chimney, but just a little left
Nor is a resurrected family sofa in the center
but just a little left.

Eh Tih Zwell

A Song for Hall House*

Pardon me, William
our birth is but a sleep and a forgetting
our life's star must cut through
unceased thinging of girlchild and
constant cloaking boykindness
in perpetual loudest
biggest meanest richest
fastest most painful
Night terrors neglect abuse
800 million watt searchlights
guide their prance
O Star! Shine through!
Shine through it!

Heaven's a way of looking at earth:
the wings of the mop rag, gathering in
mirror the angels'.

Hall House was a home for neglected and delinquent children.

Eh Tih Zwell

Away from the Mess

The Sunday *New York Times* was on the porch unread.
Waking early and thinking to tidy bedside accumulata
before adding more. I saw a sick story
on the front of the Style section
I'd planned to toss last week.
Style is of no use to me.

But soon inside was Vicki Robin
in Seattle, talking and listening
talking and listening, talking and listening and listening
and listening more
waiting like a hawk at dawn
hoping the world will renew
itself, helping it along.

Folding the paper neatly around the article,
I opened the drapes this dark February morning
to come downstairs to write a book on nonviolence.
Turned out the light, then knew it mistaken
to leave anything valuable on a bed to be collapsed in
    later,
the article must live on the mantle. I lifted it in the dark
turned to the mantle and at a hand's glance
the oval mirror perched there rolled eastward.

An irregular ovalling rolling mirror, Victorian
paste flowers on wood, once gold, now black
Florentine from Florence, Great-great Aunt Nellie
    Crowther's
is going off the dark mantle, to the radiator, to the floor
breaking, sure to be a big crappy mess
the sort I make quite well.

So it went, but didn't break, only the frame.
When I got the light back on
there was my face
looking down
laughing right in it.

Downstairs at my desk
near dawn,
an outline of a huge black bird
sought the corner of my eye.
I watched it
fly slow like an owl
only too small-headed.
Finally, a hawk
lazily waking, lifting
up and down a few feet limb to limb
in a dead walnut choked by ivy
cleaning its feathers
as slow as it pleased.

I lost the wakening hawk
on the neighbor's lawn
then in the habit of staring
I saw
the snow begin.

Faint blurs on the window
swiftly grew heavy, deep, glorious
in minutes, piled thick
on every branch, singing

"Celebrate loft in the pine trees.
Glorify all the pines welcome.
Smile and seat whoever comes."

Hawks know snow.

For Marilyn Welker and Vicki Robin, Feb 17, 2002

Listening

Mother Time
walks ahead
sweeping the flagstones
her broom back and forth
back and forth
back and forth

I heard Mother speak in the garden today
I don't know what she wanted to say
But I think she was happy, most happy to see
I think she was happy with me.

I heard Mother speak in the garden today
the flowers in her voice, the leaves its inflection
branches of meaning directed to me
"Sit and be happy, rest and be free."

Toil was her first name, work was her last
and in her mold my own span was cast
Effort required every day of one's life
for justice and equity, struggle and strife

I heard Mother speak in the garden today
"Sit and be happy; rest and be free."

The Hopewell

Maybe they were just like us

Crying

for order
safety
a great leader
and when they had one

at last
and that sage or leader passed

no trains, no cathedrals
no televised choirs
echoing off stone
carved to look like silk
and built to astonish

but only earth
basket after basket

basket after basket of earth,

arranged to tell
leader Moon where
to come next time,

where to deliver
her earthly assistant
who would bring
order again—

Maybe.

Notes

Eh Tih Zwell is 'singing spelling' for the first three words of the chorus in the hymn "It Is Well With My Soul." Susie Hammond Locklear, Music Director at the First Presbyterian Church of Chillicothe, often shows the choir alternate spellings to keep in the mind's eye, so the audience hears the meaning of the words more clearly. Try it both ways, and see for yourself.

Ellin Eastwood Sucheston Carter founded the Women's Poetry Workshop (WPW) at Ohio State University in June, 1975 and led its meetings until 2003. During this period, fourteen other poetry cooperatives formed in Ohio following the WPW example of cooperative sharing and open, free public readings. (*Ellin Carter at Highbank Farm, 1964*, page 57; *Women's Poetry Workshop*, page 61; *Memorial Salad*, page 73)

Bruce Lombardo (1956-2017), conservation biologist and communications expert, who shared science joyfully with the public on two continents—at Hopewell Culture National Historic Park in summer and Africa in winter. In Mozambique he led efforts to save rhinoceros, wild dogs, and other endangered species. Nancy Stranahan, Founder of the Arc of Appalachia, was his spouse and partner in preservation. (*To Bruce Lombardo on His Way to Heaven*, page 23)

Also by Kezia Sproat

"A Reappraisal of Shakespeare's View of Women." Columbus, OH: dissertation, Ohio State University, 1975.

"Re-reading *Othello*, II, 1." *The Kenyon Review*, 7(3), 44-51. 1985.

The National Longitudinal Surveys of Labor Market Experience: An Annotated Bibliography of Research (with Helene Churchill and Carol Sheets). Lexington, MA, D.C. Heath, 1985. First produced at The Ohio State University Center for Human Resource Research.

Kezia, circa 1969. Photo by Dorothy Cameron

A Short Course in Nonviolence. Chillicothe, OH: Highbank Farm Peace Education Center, 2001.

[Editor] *In Tune with the River, A Part of the Bridge*, Collected Poems of Ellin Carter. Columbus, OH: Women's Poetry Workshop, 2007.

Beginning Nonviolence: Learning and Teaching Nonviolence To Use Everyday (with John Looney). Galena, OH: Skye's the Limit Publishing & Public Relations, LLC, 2013.

Tuwyn — Poems by Kezia Sproat. Galena, OH: Skye's the Limit Publishing & Public Relations, LLC, 2018.

www.ingramcontent.com/pod-product-compliance
Lightning Source LLC
Chambersburg PA
CBHW071304040426
42444CB00009B/1867